All about you

Who are your friends?

Jillian Powell

Wayland

All about you

Where did you come from?
Who are you?
Who are your family?
Who are your friends?

Picture acknowledgements

The publishers would like to thank the following for allowing their photographs to be reproduced in this book: Angus Blackburn 19, 27; Chapel Studios 28 (below/Zul); Skjold 9; Tony Stone Worldwide 17 (Terry Vine); Reflections (Jennie Woodcock) *title page*, 8 (below), 12 (above), 15, 20, 21 (above), 24 (below), 25, 26, 28 (above); Wayland Picture Library 16 (both), 22; Tim Woodcock Picture Library *cover*, 4, 5, 11, 13, 18 (both); ZEFA 7 (below), 8 (above), 10, 12 (below), 21 (below), 23 (above).

Series editor: Francesca Motisi
Editors: Joan Walters and Francesca Motisi
Series designer: Jean Wheeler

This edition published in 1996 by
Wayland (Publishers) Ltd

First published in 1993 by
Wayland (Publishers) Limited
61, Western Road, Hove
East Sussex, BN3 1JD England

British Library Cataloguing in Publication Data
Powell, Jillian
Who are your Friends? – (All About You Series)
I. Title   II. Series
306.85

HARDBACK ISBN 0-7502-0789-2

PAPERBACK ISBN 0-7502-1892-4

Typeset by Dorchester Typesetting Group Limited
Printed and bound by Rotolito Lombarda S.p.A., Milan, Italy

Contents

Friends are people who like one another and like spending time together.

Who are your friends?

All kinds of people can
become friends.

Old people can
be good friends
with young
people.

Friends often like the same music, books, films or clothes.

You can share things, or swap things with friends.

You can have fun with friends,
playing games or sharing
your toys.

Friends can help each other
make and build things.

Friends often spend weekends or holidays together.

They might go out to a park, cinema or **museum**, or just stay home and watch their favourite television programmes.

Friends sometimes get to know one another because they are **neighbours** or because they go to the same school.

Where did you meet your friends?

Sometimes, when you move house or go to a new school, you can feel a bit **lonely** until you meet new friends.

New friends make us feel happy.

You make
new friends
by talking
and getting
to know
one another.

You find out you like doing the same things and you like being together.

Friends can share **secrets**. You can tell a good friend things you wouldn't tell anyone else.

20

Friends can share jokes too!

You can tell friends if you are unhappy or in trouble. They will try to help you and you can sometimes help them.

Helping each other makes friends feel good.

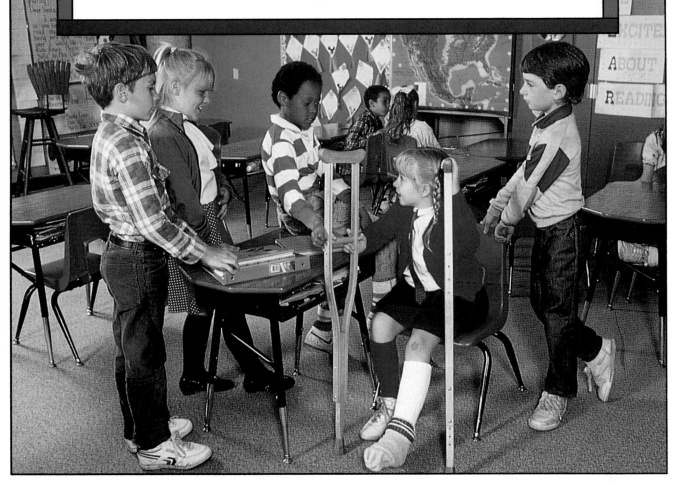

You don't always agree with friends or with things they do.

Sometimes friends may **quarrel**.

But good friends soon **forgive** each other and make up.

Friends often spend special days like birthdays together.

You might have a party and invite all your friends, or go out for a treat.

When friends move away, they can stay in touch by telephone, or by sending cards and letters.

Some friends
stay friends
for years.

Notes for parents and teachers

Maths
● Measurement and number: measuring and comparing physical dimensions and attributes of friends not only provides ample opportunities for number work, it also leads into a discussion about standard and non-standard units of measurement.
● Data handling: data could be collected about who has female, male, or both, as friends. The results could be expressed as a Venn diagram.
● Enter and access data on computer database e.g. 'Our facts'.

Language
● Expressions relating to 'friends' could be collected and discussed: 'A friend in need is a friend indeed'; 'With friends like hers, who needs enemies?' 'Who goes there: friend or foe?' Children could write stories illustrating the meanings.
● Writing stories about 'My Best Friend'. Why is my friend my friend? What makes a good friend? Good friends 'recipes': 'a tablespoon of kindness; a teaspoon of helpfulness; a pinch of humour' etc.
● Children can explore the topic of friendship through story: pets and animals as friends.
● The writing of letters to friends who are far away. (See pen-friends Geography)

Music
● Songs that have 'friendship' as a theme: singing and listening/appreciating e.g. Carole King's *You've Got a Friend.*
● Composition: friends could compose a 'sympathetic' piece of music – perhaps one that involved a 'call' from one friend and an 'answer' from the other.

History
● Famous friends in history (and Literature): Queen Elizabeth I and Sir Francis Drake; Anthony and Cleopatra (fact or fiction?); Batman and Robin etc.
● Time-lines: How long have you known your best friend? What have you done together over the years?

Science
● An exploration of what it might mean to be a 'friend of the Earth' might open up a discussion about: conservation/ecology; preserving habitats/animal species; tropical rain forest destruction; pollution; recycling; alternative sources of power etc.
● 'Animal friends': symbiosis – the special and close relationship between two organisms of different species that live together and gain from their interaction e.g. ox-pecker birds and antelopes; pilot-fish and sharks.

Art and Craft
● Life-size paintings of a friend can be created by working in pairs and drawing round one another. These can be cut out and displayed. Parts of the body can be labelled.
● Silhouette pictures can be created by drawing around the silhouetted shadow (using an overhead projector) of a friend's profile on black paper with a white pencil. These can then be cut out and displayed as a 'guess who?' gallery. There could be written clues from the other children by way of the 'positive attributes' mentioned under Multicultural R.E./ Health.

Technology
● Friends could work together collaboratively to design, make and evaluate a toy of some kind from suitable materials.

P.E./Dance/Drama
● Children could be taught a range of co-operative games e.g. 'Stick in the Mud' where everyone except the catcher/s not only tries to avoid being caught, but actively tries to 'free' those that have been caught.
● Children could be encouraged to work out a dance with a friend or friends which 'tells the story' of their friendship.
● Drama: acting out in small groups some action showing: a) the sort of behaviour you might expect from a good friend b) the sort of behaviour you would not expect from a good friend.
● Role-play: 'the new girl or boy at school'.

Geography
● Pen-friends at a school in a different town or country would encourage an interesting exchange of letters between children (see Language). Finding out things about the other school. Where is it? How does it compare with one's own school?
● Mapping: where do my friends live? What is the route to their house?

Multicultural/R.E./Health
● Positive attributes: Two or three children from a class could be chosen each day. The other children are invited to write down two things they like about each person. These can be displayed with the silhouetted portraits mentioned under Art and Craft.
● How do my friends help me? A focus on the positive things a friend can provide, and the principle of mutual support and the responsibility that goes with this.
● Do I always do what my friends do? What should one do if a friend does something one disapproves of? Discuss.

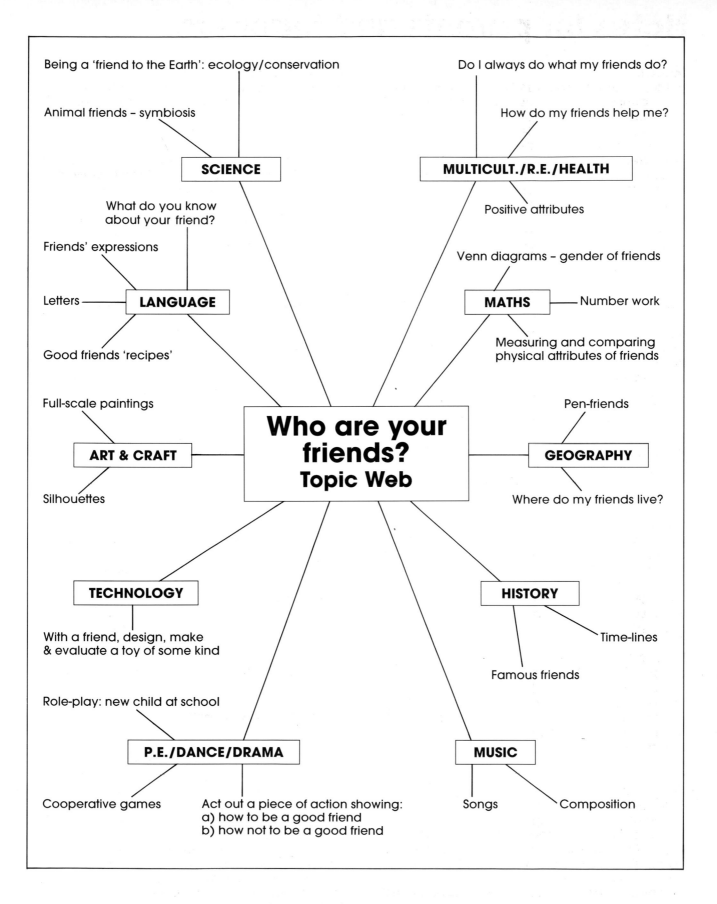

Being a 'friend to the Earth': ecology/conservation

Animal friends – symbiosis

SCIENCE

What do you know about your friend?

Friends' expressions

Letters —— **LANGUAGE**

Good friends 'recipes'

Full-scale paintings

ART & CRAFT

Silhouettes

TECHNOLOGY

With a friend, design, make & evaluate a toy of some kind

Role-play: new child at school

P.E./DANCE/DRAMA

Cooperative games

Act out a piece of action showing:
a) how to be a good friend
b) how not to be a good friend

Who are your friends?
Topic Web

Do I always do what my friends do?

How do my friends help me?

MULTICULT./R.E./HEALTH

Positive attributes

Venn diagrams – gender of friends

MATHS —— Number work

Measuring and comparing physical attributes of friends

Pen-friends

GEOGRAPHY

Where do my friends live?

HISTORY

Time-lines

Famous friends

MUSIC

Songs   Composition

31

Glossary

Forgive To forget that you have argued and to be friends again.

Lonely To feel alone and without friends.

Museum A building where you can see very old things from history, art and science.

Neighbours People who live next door to your house or nearby.

Quarrel An argument.

Secrets Special things that you only tell to your friends and family.

Books to read

Your World: Your Friends
  by Michael Pollard
  (Wayland 1989)

Health and Friends
  by Dorothy Baldwin
  (Wayland 1987)

The World of Play
  by Anna Sproule
  (Macdonald 1988)

Index